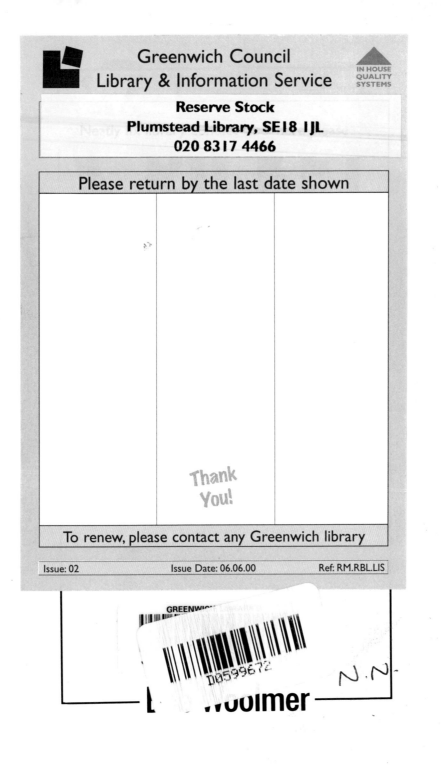

GREENWICH
I0599672

Woolmer

## A & C Black · London

GREENWICH
LIBRARIES

First published 1993 by
A & C Black (Publishers) Ltd
35 Bedford Row, London WC1R 4JH

© 1993 Bob Woolmer

ISBN 0 7136 3721 8

A CIP catalogue record for this book
is available from the British Library.

**Acknowledgements**
Thanks to the players and staff of Warwickshire
C.C.C., and in particular to Paul Smith, Piran
Holloway, Andy Moles, Alan Donald, Dermot Reeve,
Tim Munton, Roger Twose, Stuart Nottingham and
Gladstone Small for demonstrating the techniques.

Cover photograph courtesy of Allsport (UK) Ltd.
All other photographs by Sylvio Dokov.
Illustrations by Taurus Graphics.

Typeset, printed and bound in Great Britain by
Latimer Trend & Co. Ltd., Plymouth

# CONTENTS

I dedicate this book to my father, who christened me with bat and ball in my cot, and who said 'Son, I hope this will be your life'; to my mother, who encouraged me and endured hours of golf-ball and tennis-ball cricket against our garage door; to the Bickmores at Yardley Court School, who suffered my academic moods around the beloved game; to the late Colin Page and to Colin Cowdrey, for their patience and words of inspiration; to Alan Knott, a brilliant wicket-keeper and a great student of the game; and finally to my wife and family, for their love, patience and understanding of my passion.

# FOREWORD

I was lucky enough to come under the eye of Sir Jack Hobbs at an early age. He was the master batsman of his era, with a method and technique that would stand the test of time and make him arguably the most complete batsman, on all wickets, that the game has known.

During the first morning of the Oval Test match in 1956, he came to find me in the dressing room soon after I had been dismissed first ball. He brought me enormous encouragement at an important moment of my career and left me with the wisest piece of cricket advice that I was ever given.

'At the end of every season, before you put your cricket bag away for the Winter, take time out to analyse every facet of your game. Acknowledge the strong points and determine to build on those and improve them still further. But single out one or two weaknesses and determine to wrestle with them at the first available practice in the New Year. Work away, quite single mindedly, to put them right, and don't give up until you are satisfied that the problem is behind you. It may take you more than one season.'

He went on to say: 'Never let a season finish without the discipline of this approach to your game. If you do this I think that you are good enough to play at the top level for a long time.'

This excellent coaching book from Bob Woolmer is just the aid that I would have loved at my side each September throughout my cricket career. It would have saved me a great deal of time and anguish.

I have enjoyed watching Bob Woolmer's progress from an outstanding schoolboy cricketer, to a fine all-rounder with Kent, working on his batting technique with such single-minded zeal as to win himself a place in the England team. Everyone admired his dedicated approach and enthusiasm for the game.

Bob Woolmer's strength was his determination to keep looking for ways in which he could adapt and improve his game, both as a bowler and a batsman. He understands more than most players I have played with that you cannot afford to stand still: the game soon overtakes you if you are not alert to change.

With this book the author brings to the art of cricket a high quality contribution which will generate enormous interest and be of great value to cricketers as they strive and aspire to the top.

*Colin Cowdrey*

**Sir Colin Cowdrey CBE**

# INTRODUCTION

In 1983 I suffered a back injury which eventually terminated my professional playing career in May the following year. It was a shock to the system, a totally alien experience to be suddenly shut off from something that I really loved. However, the premature end to my playing days did provide me with the stimulus to embark on a coaching career, something that I had wanted to do for some time. Ever since, cricket coaching has brought me rich dividends, even if it hasn't made me a fortune!

The real riches to be gleaned from cricket coaching are the day-to-day experiences of dealing with cricketers. To devote hours to one player in attempting to iron out his technical deficiencies in, say, driving, and then to see that player go out into the middle and execute that shot perfectly hour after hour, compiling a century in the process, gives a coach a special thrill.

The more coaching of players that I experienced, the more I wanted to record what I had learnt and what I try to teach. I wanted to compile some kind of reference work for the future, just like the coaching manual by Trevor Bailey that I had found so useful in the early days.

I hope that *Skilful Cricket* manages to impart at least some of the knowledge that I have accumulated over my many years of watching, playing with and coaching some of the world's finest cricketers. I hope that I can help young and aspiring players in explaining to them that it is possible to circumvent some of the rocky paths of poor technique on the route to technical proficiency.

You will find many more comprehensive works on the subtleties of batting, swing bowling, leg-spin bowling and wicket-keeping. But my hope is that you will not come across many more *useful* and *practical* publications than this; useful to all levels of the cricketing fraternity, and practical whether you bat, bowl, field in the slips or keep wicket.

Enjoy your cricket!

**Bob Woolmer**

*Note* Throughout the book players are referred to individually as 'he'. This should, of course, be taken to mean 'he or she' where appropriate.

# EQUIPMENT

One of the basic requirements for a cricketer is his equipment. I knew a young professional bowler who went overseas for a Winter with only one pair of bowling boots. Half-way through the season his boots split and every week-end he had to patch them up with tape. The young man was very lucky that he didn't do irreparable harm to his ankles or feet. I also remember being told early in my career to have two pairs of boots and, in fact, two of everything in my bag. I know that this does not make *economic* sense in many cases, but it makes common sense if you are playing regularly.

Choosing a bat is also very important and there are one or two tips that might help. Firstly, don't select a bat that is too big or too heavy for you, but remember you can change the balance by adding another rubber grip to the handle. Try to look at the grain of the bat: narrow grains are usually better than wide grain bats. I would always look for a bat with 12 grains visible. If possible, bounce a ball on the bat and listen to the noise it makes: the harder the sound, the more it will need 'knocking in'; the softer it sounds, the quicker you will be able to use it, but you are likely to get surface dents or hairline cracks which are not dangerous but actually a sign of a good 'stick'.

Having chosen a bat and assuming it is not covered with the modern polyurethane covers and/or laminates, you will need to oil the bat with raw linseed oil twice before use, applying the oil as you might apply after-shave lotion. Apply it only to the surface you might use and to areas of the bat that will make contact with the ground during an innings (the bottom and the 'V' at the bottom of the back of the bat where you might hit down the wicket when putting back divots on a wet surface). Be careful not to expose the bat to wet ground because the bottom of the bat will swell, making it look ugly. This will subside as it dries, but will need sanding down and re-oiling.

'Knocking in' a bat is also important. I preferred to knock it in the middle but then I was sponsored and had a supply of bats. Alternatively, put a ball in a sock and continually bang it on the bat.

How do you know if a bat is the correct size? Essentially, if the bat is the same size as your inside leg trouser measurement you won't go far wrong. The suitable weight can be gauged by seeing if you can hold the bat with your top hand parallel to the ground for 45 seconds!

Look at Paul Smith the batsman (fig. 1). His pads meet the modern front and inside leg thigh pads and abdominal protector, all now contained in a special unit. He is wearing batting gloves which should have soft leather palms and, more importantly, good protection for the fingers. There are a lot of gloves on the market, all of which are good, but look particularly for the protection on the thumb and first finger of the bottom hand, which are the two areas that are most vulnerable.

A chest guard is useful for particular wickets and types of bowler, as is a helmet with visor. The main reason that the professional cricketer wears this much protective equipment is his very professionalism; missing a game through injury could mean loss of a place in the side or loss of income. The well-protected amateur need not miss any cricket during the season. For the younger cricketer who has to play against more senior players, it will increase confidence. Don't be conned by the sissy image!

All this equipment is not cheap; decisions may be conditioned by costs.

Certain techniques can help and stop you from being hit. I remember having great confidence in my batting technique against quick bowlers, and during my career being hit only once, by Malcolm Marshall, but it prevented me playing for six weeks! Over to you . . .

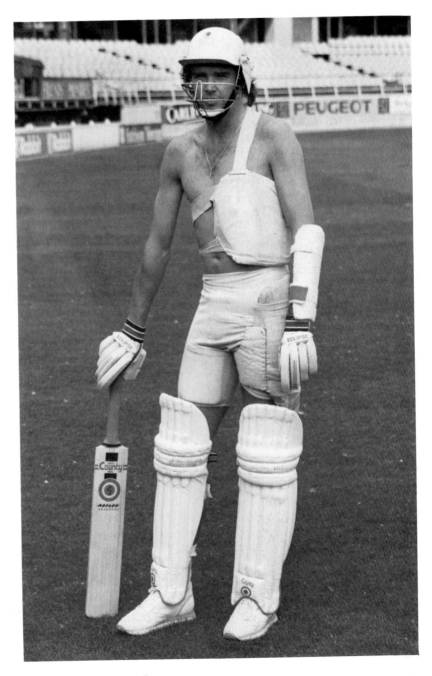

**Fig. 1 Batsman's equipment**

# TAKING GUARD

## Leg-stump

This guard is favoured by the better players. It will give them room to hit the ball. It does mean that they must know exactly where their off-stump is. I would recommend adopting this guard when facing in-swing bowlers and off-spinners on a turning wicket.

## Middle-and-leg or 'two legs'

This is a guard favoured by players who enjoy playing on both sides of the wicket. It makes them feel more aware of where their off-stump is. Used primarily on good wickets.

Fig. 2   Leg-stump guard

Fig. 3   Middle-and-leg guard

# Middle or centre

This guard favours on-side players and weak off-side players. The majority of runs would come on the leg side: psychologically bowlers cannot see the stumps and they may get frustrated. However, players who take this guard are often susceptible to LBW decisions.

**Fig. 4  Middle-stump guard**

# GRIP

The way in which a cricket bat is held in the hands has become the subject of much debate in recent years. The primary reason for this is the advent of the incessant battery of batsmen from fast, intimidatory bowling. Another reason is the need in modern one-day cricket to adapt and improvise the strokes played in order to accommodate the crash-bang-wallop requirements of limited-overs matches. The scope of this book lies in highlighting what is basically sound.

**Fig. 5 The basic grip**

## Basic grip

The position of the hands on the bat handle will vary according to the type of bat used, its length of handle, its weight, and the strength of the user. Having said that, the basic position should always be held up as an ideal. The hands should meet half-way up the handle (*see* fig. 5). The natural 'V' formed by the thumb and first finger of both hands should be aligned just off centre towards the outside edge of the bat. The top hand should be holding the bat firmly, while the bottom hand should be relaxed in holding the bat as you might hold a young bird. The role of the bottom hand becomes crucial in any discussion of shot-making (*see* later).

## Alternatives

Fig. 6 below shows the adjusted grip used initially by Alan Knott in order to cope with the Australian pace attack of Lillee and Thomson during the 1974/75 series Down Under. The grip helped Knott to play 'high' in an effort to accommodate the excessive pace and bounce that these two bowlers were generating on the green and generally uneven pitches on which the series was played. The one drawback was that the method restricted his ability to drive the ball straight powerfully: because the grip 'choked' the free-flowing movement of the straight drive, Knott found himself push-driving for a single or two runs,

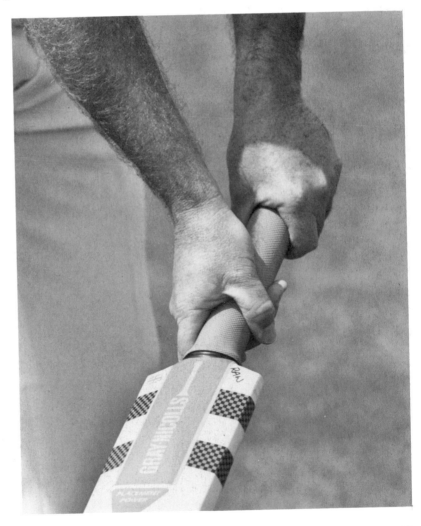

**Fig. 6   Alan Knott's adjusted grip**

instead of drilling the ball to the boundary rope.

The evolution of the method begun in front of a long mirror, more usually used to check that one's attire is in order, but now pressed into service as an old-fashioned video play-back machine! Visualising the bounce of the ball, Knott studied the response of his hands as he adjusted the height of the bat. The first problem he encountered with the orthodox grip was that he could only reach a certain height. Therefore, he was inhibited in dealing with the ball that, in cricket parlance, 'gets big', i.e. rises disconcertingly (for the batsman!) off the pitch, too quickly to be hooked. By adjusting his grip he found he could 'periscope' up another foot, which made the rising delivery playable. It ought to be noted by sceptics of this theory that the pace and bounce generated by these two great bowlers were such that the length that the ball was rising from was not short enough for the batsman to duck underneath, which would probably have been an easier solution!

This considered method helped Alan Knott to play some fine innings during his career. For a good many players who listened to him and tried it for themselves (myself included), it was a great help in the struggle to come to terms with ultra-quick bowling. Should any batsman reading this book wish to adopt this method, it should be realised that it does cut down on a batsman's ability to play a wide range of shots. However, this might be a blessing if a batsman is impetuous during the early stages of an innings and is guilty of playing too many adventurous shots too early. In fact, one might consider it as a method of starting to build an innings!

# STANCE

In all stances what should be stressed is that the batsman must be comfortable, he must be able to move backwards or forwards without hindrance, and he must be relaxed. Keep your eyes level and transfer your body weight slightly forwards: it is easier to go back by rocking off the front foot. Work out your own method and practise it until you are happy.

## Feet close together

Very few batsmen now adopt this stance because it reduces balance.

## Orthodox

Feet shoulder-width apart, parallel to the crease; hands resting on the front pad; bat resting on the ground; head, shoulder and front hip over the front foot; eyes level; front elbow pointing down the wicket; knees bent to allow movement forwards or backwards. This is probably the best way to start.

Fig. 7   Stance: feet close together

Fig. 8   Orthodox stance

# Feet wide apart

This is a stance favoured by the great South African batsman Graeme Pollock, and adopted by a number of cricketers. Notice that the feet are wide apart and the bat is resting in between the feet. The theory behind this particular stance is that the batsman will have to move less to get to the ball, so eliminating movement-orientated errors. To play forwards means only sideways adjustment, and playing back is initiated by rocking back off the front foot. If practised and thoroughly understood, this can be a very effective method.

# Open

The open stance has been adopted by a number of very great cricketers, such as Ken Barrington, Jim Parks and to the nth degree by Peter Willey. The theory behind this stance is that it gives the batsman a better view of the ball and makes him stronger on the leg side. The pitfalls are that he has a long way to go in order to drive an off-side half-volley, and he is too square-on, limiting the number of shots on the off side. A good deal of practice and playing to your limitations can make this an acceptable technique.

**Fig. 9   Stance: feet wide apart**

**Fig. 10  Stance: high back-lift**

## High back-lift

Here is the modern stance pioneered by Tony Greig, and adopted by Mike Brearley, Graham Gooch and many other first-class cricketers. The theory here is that it helps the batsman to be properly balanced, to play the rising ball more easily and to stop him from toppling towards the off side, thereby preventing LBW decisions. It can make the batsman susceptible to the yorker, but it is restful on the back!

# Rhythm

How do I play *really* fast bowling? I can't play spinners! My feet won't move properly! I am not picking up the ball!

What causes the above statements and questions? Just as bowlers need rhythm, so do batsmen. So how do you achieve batting rhythm? Many coaches will tell you that you must stand still in order to judge line and length correctly, and they are absolutely correct. In fact, if there is a key to successful batting then this is it. But how can you stay still when Frank Tyson, Michael Holding or Fred Trueman are hurling down thunderbolts? The answer is you can't. You will have to develop a technique that gives you time to play these bowlers. And rhythm helps you. Batting rhythm is created by making feet movements fractionally before the bowler releases the ball. There are many such movements.

● Moving the back foot back and across towards the off-stump and bringing the weight back to the front foot as the bowler releases the ball ('still' while judging length), and then making the final movement, having judged length, and playing the appropriate shot.

● Moving the front foot forwards a fraction just before the bowler bowls, initiating your movements and response to the delivery as above.

● Picking up the back foot and front foot and spreading them a little wider, without sideways movement, again just before release, and once more initiating movement.

These are three ways in which rhythm is generated. These methods have to be practised and used at the start of an innings because if you are lucky enough to get to a hundred, you'll find that you'll be standing perfectly still and the ball will be looking as big as a football. I often found that I could use all three techniques comfortably depending on how I felt on the day! You must be prepared to practise and work on whichever one suits you.

# FORWARD DEFENSIVE SHOT

This shot provides the base from which most innings are built.

I have often read and heard in discussion that teaching the forward defensive shot to a young cricketer may dampen his enthusiasm for the game. I cannot agree: in my opinion it is tantamount to learning to ski without knowing how to stop! I would also venture to suggest that without this skill very few innings would last any length of time.

I wish to be the last person to discourage a young player from hitting the ball. By the nature of the game runs are vital to a side. However, if bowlers are encouraged to bowl on a good length then batsmen will have to meet that delivery with the appropriate shot.

This being the case, the argument for learning the forward defensive is very strong. I was once told that during a century innings, the forward defensive was used for nearly 70% of that innings. While I personally have never made a study of this statistic, I am perfectly prepared to believe it. So, always start with the forward defensive stroke.

Defending a 9in target from a $5\frac{1}{2}$oz missile not much bigger than a bar of soap, with a 2lb 8oz bat, 36in long, seems in retrospect a pretty easy thing to do. In fact, it is a good deal harder than one initially expects. Study the photographs here and practise, by shadow or mirror imagery, the various stages, and then with the ball in degrees of progression. Remember: judgement of length is vital. If an error occurs, remember also: 'If in doubt – Push out!'

Playing with 'soft' hands could make the difference between being caught at slip and the ball not carrying, especially against the turning ball. Practise in front of a mirror or with the aid of a video camera.

Above all, try to 'feel' the necessary positions in order to correct faults when in the middle or at net practices.

## Front view

Fig. 11   Eyes level; pick up the bat before the bowler bowls; watch the ball from the bowler's hand and pick the length and line as soon as possible

Fig. 12   As you step forwards, rotate your front shoulder towards the ball; allow enough room with your front foot to let the path of the bat meet the ball's path

Fig. 13   Ensure the bat is straight and that the bottom of the bat rests against the front pad; also ensure that the hands are above the ball and that the eyes draw an imaginary line through them to the ball

Fig. 11

## Side view

Fig. 14   Bottom hand above the top hand on the back-lift; face slightly open; top hand taken back over the back knee; balance of weight favouring the front leg – a good guide would be feeling your front hip over your front foot; head and shoulder together

Fig. 15   Stride forwards towards the line of the ball, using your back foot for propulsion and ensuring that the front leg is the main weight-bearing leg so that the balance is not tipped backwards; head over the front foot; a common fault is that the heel of the back foot is grounded, causing poor balance

Fig. 16   Make sure the bat travels parallel to the initial shoulder shape; note that the top hand is in front of the bottom hand – this will keep the ball down; ensure that the front elbow is high, which will induce a straight bat; finally, release the bottom hand grip so that only the thumb and forefinger have control

Fig. 14

Fig. 12

Fig. 13

Fig. 15

Fig. 16

# BACKWARD DEFENSIVE SHOT

The short rising delivery is more in vogue in today's game than at any other time in the history of the sport, except perhaps for the 'Bodyline Tour' of 1932–3.

Many young cricketers have been 'found out' at the higher levels because of their inability to cope with the rising ball. Again, study the photographs here carefully because the orthodox method is added to by other methods of dealing with the delivery. ('Getting big' is cricket terminology for steep bounce from just short of a length.)

Fig. 17   From the stance position, go back and across your stumps to the off-stump but no further – remember, the short delivery is designed to get you out in the slips, at short leg or in the gully; keep your back foot parallel to the batting crease; draw the front leg back to the heel of the back foot, and rest on the toe to create balance; again, stay sideways-on until the bat has had a chance to come through

Fig. 18   Bring the hands through parallel to your shoulders and above the height of the ball, using a cradling motion, both arms being bent – only then will the shoulders turn slightly; play the ball at waist height, making sure that the top hand is in front of the bottom hand and that the bottom hand is again in the thumb-and-forefinger position; ensure that the front elbow is high to create a straight bat

Fig. 19 Depending on how high the ball bounces, you may be forced to 'periscope' the bat higher to deal with steep bounce; this is achieved by releasing the top hand grip and allowing the bat to be lifted above your eye level; please note the bottom hand thumb and forefinger grip ideally exposed in this frame

# AVOIDING THE BOUNCER

Fig. 20 Avoiding the bouncer: swaying

Whatever method you may have developed to avoid the ball by swaying or ducking, remember that at all times keep your eye on the ball. Make sure that your weight does not move on to the back foot because this will restrict your movement and could cause you to get hit.

The backward defensive shot and swaying or ducking out of the way are the defensive methods of keeping out the bouncing ball. Quite often you have probably heard that attack is the best form of defence. You may wish to take on the bowler and hook him to the boundary . . .

**Fig. 21   Avoiding the bouncer: ducking**

# HOOK SHOT

Play the hook to a bouncer or short-pitched delivery aimed at your head. This is a risk shot and you must be confident before taking on a quick bowler. Attempting to hit the ball too hard can cause many problems. Use the pace of the bowler. Try to stay in control of the shot and watch out for the ball bouncing too high. If that is the case, bale out of the shot by swinging the hands down very quickly as you swivel.

In order to hook or pull (*see* page 39) any ball your reactions must be quick. Transfer your weight from the front foot to the back foot, but at the same time keep the balance slightly forwards of centre. Keep your head and eyes very still.

The advent of the helmet has made this shot less of a risk. However it is still often played poorly, helmet or no helmet.

**Fig. 22   Try to get your body inside the line of the ball, with your hands as high as possible in the back-lift**

**Fig. 23  Make contact with your arms straight and parallel to the ground**

**Fig. 24  As you make contact, swivel on your feet, keeping the arms straight**

# FRONT AND BACK FOOT DRIVES

Fig. 25  Head level; weight balanced; front hip over front foot – ideal position to pick length

Fig. 26  The ball is short and about a foot wide of the off-stump; the batsman has stepped back and across as if to play the backward defensive shot, his front shoulder aiming at the ball; the key to this shot – the batsman has chosen to attack; notice the rotation of the shoulders – this will provide the necessary swing and power for the shot

Driving a ball is surely one of the great sensations of batting. Judgement of length is again vital; a half-volley is easily mistaken and often causes early dismissal. It is essential that when you practise these shots you spend time 'grooving' the shot by repetitive practice. Again, study the photographs and work on attaining the right shape; over-exaggerate if necessary.

# Drive off the back foot

This shot is played to a ball that pitches short of a good length, but that is relatively close to the body, giving no room to cut. However, the ball is short enough to punish and many coaches look for this shot as a sign of class in young batsmen.

This shot should be played as much as possible in the 'V' between mid-wicket and extra cover. The natural angle of the delivery will make the ball go square but you would be ill-advised to play this shot square of the wicket, a catch behind being the most obvious result.

**Fig. 27  Impact; hands high over the ball; bat very straight due to the front elbow being in such a correct position**

**Fig. 28  Punchy follow-through; body lifted by being on the toes; bat remains exactly on line with the ball**

# Drive off the front foot

This shot is played to a ball of full length, usually a half-volley or a full toss. It is sometimes played 'on the up' to a good length delivery, depending on the state of the wicket.

Keeping the back foot still, use it as a compass point and move the front foot around in a semi-circle. You will discover that every drive can be played from point to mid-wicket using the same principles.

Remember, when hitting 'on the up', the push drive is safer only if you are prepared to hit in the 'V' between mid-off and mid-on, and play much closer to the front leg to prevent being bowled through the gate.

Practice and grooving are vital for the drives. It is the best shot to play and the hardest to perfect.

**Fig. 29**

**Fig. 29** The front foot has moved down the wicket to the pitch of the ball, with the toes pointing at the ball; leave yourself enough room in order to let the hands swing through; if you get too close to the ball you will find that you will play an in-to-out drive, losing power and being more likely to edge the ball to slip; the shoulder line is pointing directly at the ball; note also the line the shoulders draw – it will be important to swing along this line

**Fig. 30** It is important to remember that the drive is a swing as opposed to a punch; moments before impact the arms need to extend back, taking the hands back; again, the shoulder turn is vital – it creates the power and timing; the front arm is almost straight and is about to lead the bottom hand through the shot; remember, the shot is a *swing*

**Fig. 31** Impact; hands over the ball; arms straight; wrists slightly cocked to create a straight bat; hip over the front foot; balancing on a lifted back foot; notice the room necessary to make this shot (I do not advocate this technique when playing 'on the up': remember, this is a half-volley)

**Fig. 32** Part 1 of the follow-through; the hands have stayed on the original shoulder line; the arms are extended ready for the wrist turn as depicted in fig. 34

**Fig. 33** Part 2 of the follow-through – the 'Cowdrey' or 'stop' follow through; again, the hands have stayed on line and pushed forwards through and over the ball

**Fig. 34** Completion of follow through

**Fig. 30**

**Fig. 31**

**Fig. 32**

**Fig. 33**

**Fig. 34**

# Coming out to drive

Coming down the wicket to drive can create unnecessary risks if not performed properly. For example, should you get on the wrong side of the ball or too far away from it, you could be stumped. So it is very important to remember the following principles.

When you come down, do so *at the ball*, i.e. just after the ball has been released. Come down slowly to start with and be prepared to defend if you have to; if the ball is in the correct place, then you can hit safely over the top or along the ground. The four movements necessary and highlighted by the photographs should be practised regularly and often, as you would any other particular shot.

- The **first** movement is a long step towards the ball. (*See* fig. 35.)

- The **second** movement is called the 'chassis' – the back foot passes the right foot. This has the advantage of keeping the eyes level as you come down the wicket. (*See* fig. 36.)

- The **third** movement is another large stride with the front foot using your hip weight to come over the top of the front leg so that you are now in the perfect position in which to hit the ball. (*See* fig. 37.)

If the ball is a half-volley then by all means go ahead and hit it – your momentum will carry the ball a long way should you want to hit it for six. If you do want to hit it for six, lean back slightly as in fig. 38. If you're not to the pitch of the ball, as I mentioned before, be quite prepared to play a forward defensive shot and walk back to your crease.

Keep your eyes still and watch the ball. Do not rush this shot because any error will cause you to be stumped. Many players try to hit without the normal swing associated with a drive. Remember that as you get into the shot, dip or rotate that front shoulder so that your hands can swing through the ball. If you do not dip the shoulder you will find that the right side of your body will come through the shot too quickly, and the ball will go straight up into the air . . . You're out!

Fig. 35

Fig. 36

## Glances off front and back foot

### Front foot

In this position the ball is on the line of the pads, probably just down the leg side. Its length is fairly full and you are unable to play any other shot except the glance down to fine leg. Notice in fig. 39 that the batsman's head is right over the ball. The bat, controlled by both hands, has turned and the ball has glanced off the face. Notice also that the weight is forwards and over the ball – that is critical.

**Fig. 37**

**Fig. 38**

**Fig. 39   Glance off the front foot**

## Back foot

The ball is shorter now and rising towards the hip. The batsman has gone back towards the off-stump and has turned his body square-on, with the hands in line with the front pad, where the ball should be hitting. Contact is made with the bat slightly angled, and as the completion of the shot occurs, notice in figs 40 and 41 that the left foot goes back and the body turns completely. The hands remain over the ball with the top hand in front of the bottom one. The bat has now turned. Notice that the eyes still watch the ball closely.

**Fig. 40   Glance off the back foot (1)**     **Fig. 41   Glance off the back foot (2)**

## Glance off the body

In fig. 42, the batsman is playing a glance off the body from a bouncer or a short delivery that has risen and is heading for the chest area. The weight now is lifted up on to the toes of the feet. The hands have been raised high, with the left elbow as high as possible over the top, glancing the ball down so that there is no chance of a catch at leg slip or backward short leg, or forward short leg for that matter. Again, the wrist rolls over the ball, and the top hand must stay in front of the bottom one.

**Fig. 42  Glance off the body**

# Late cut

This shot is usually played to a spinner, but can also be played to a medium pace bowler or even a quick bowler. For the sake of this particular exercise, assume that it is being played to a spinner.

It is crucial for the batsman to let the ball go past the body when playing this shot. In spotting a gap between backward point and the wicket-keeper, use the pace of the ball to run it down to third man.

Notice in fig. 43 the beginning of the shot – the batsman's toes are pointing down to third

**Fig. 43  Late cut (1)**

man, and his weight is transferred backwards towards the area in which he wishes to play the shot. The hands, again, are over the top of the ball, and the bat is raised above it. The weight is transferred to the back foot and, in fig. 44, observe how the arms straighten out and the bat goes down, hitting the ball in the direction of fine third man.

The lower the ball is, the more the knees must bend in this particular shot. In this case, the ball has bounced to quite a height. The secret of the shot is to keep the hands above the ball and to follow it down on the path it is going.

**Fig. 44  Late cut (2)**

# CROSS-BAT SHOTS

One of the main reasons for a batsman's dismissal is playing a cross-batted shot. In fact, if this type of shot is played without the necessary technique, it causes probably more errors than any other shot. The main fault stems from the bat coming down at an angle, as opposed to being horizontal or vertical.

Fig. 45 The batsman has gone back towards his middle-stump and has turned the toe of his back foot down the wicket, keeping his front shoulder in line with the ball. (The position of the back toe and the front shoulder is conditioned by the line of the ball; the back foot should be inside the line of the ball.)

Fig. 46 The front foot has now spread wide and parallel to the batting (popping) crease, creating a solid base from which to hit the ball; the front shoulder remains facing the ball

# Pull

This shot is played to a short ball delivered by a medium pace or slow bowler: the delivery that is commonly called a 'long-hop'. Played incorrectly, the pull can be fatal.

With both the pull and the cut shots, there is a problem for the predominantly right-handed left-hander in that his bottom hand is weaker. This will cause problems in the execution of the shot. For that individual so blessed it would have to be played more as a timed shot than as a power shot. Using weights to strengthen the weaker hand, and creating practice methods to enhance the shot, is also advisable.

# Cut

The cut is played to a short, wide ball. It is a great run-scoring shot but induces a large number of dismissals. (*See* over.)

**Fig. 48 (Above)** The bottom hand takes over here and the power is generated by the strong hand; the follow-through takes the weight over the front foot and, hopefully, four runs result

**Fig. 47 (Left)** Impact is in the ideal hitting area – the bat parallel to the ground, the hands above the ball, the top hand in front of the bottom hand; the arms are straight, creating maximum velocity on impact; the head and the balance are forwards of centre

# Back foot

Fig. 49 The batsman has gone back and across his stumps, with the toes of his back foot pointing down towards third man – this has kept him sideways-on, as in the back foot drive; rotate the shoulders and keep the hands high – this will create the swing; contact is made with the arms straight and in the ideal hitting area underneath the eyes; the bat and arms are parallel to the ground but fractionally above the ball; again, the bottom hand takes over and by using a throwing motion with the bottom hand and arm, excellent contact should be made

Fig. 50 The follow-through of the shot is created by rotating the wrists so that the arms maintain the line but the bat follows through along the path of the ball, which is again created by the original shoulder line; isn't coaching repetitive?

Fig. 51 Step down the wicket, keeping the body balanced and upright

Fig. 52 Rotate the shoulders to create the swing; keep the hands above the ball

## Front foot

This shot is played to a short ball, again wide outside the off-stump, normally on good wickets, against most types of bowlers, when the batsman is set and ready.

The shot is a difficult one and can lead to dismissal if played too early. Like all cross-batted shots, be wary of uneven bounce on pitches. Remember, keep the bat parallel to the ground; if not, the shot becomes more of a lottery than it already is.

Cutting over the slips is a relatively new innovation, brought about by bouncy wickets, fast bowlers and one-day cricket. I once asked Peter Kirsten what made him such a good cutter: 'If you're going to cut, cut hard' was his reply. I will add to that, if the ball is rising cut up, following the rise; if the ball is levelling out or going down, cut appropriately.

Fig. 53 (Above)  Make contact under those eyes again, with the hands at full stretch to create the maximum force

Fig. 54 (Right)  Follow through by rotating the wrists and allowing the momentum of the shot to pull the weight forwards on to the front knee, which bends to keep the balance correct

# Orthodox sweep

Oh woe is me for coaching this shot! The sweep is a dangerous shot! The batsman must invariably play across the line of the ball. Umpires often give batsmen out for playing it because they don't *like* the shot. But ask any spin bowler what he thinks of it and he will tell you that if played well, it is very difficult to contain the batsman: the shot does have the effect of messing up a spin bowler's length. So here goes . . .

The orthodox sweep is played to a good length delivery from a slow bowler (usually). I did have it played by Mushtaq Mohammed off my medium pace seamers early in my career.

There are a number of varieties of this shot: the position of the front foot can help you place the ball in different areas. If you get the front foot inside the line, you will be able to guide the ball fine. If you stay leg side of the ball, you will be able to hit squarer, and so on. If you are scared of going down the wicket to the spinner, change his length by sweeping him to improve your run-scoring ability against the turning ball. But beware of very bouncy wickets.

Fig. 55  Having picked the length, step forwards and bend down low; back knee on the ground; turn the shoulder into line with the ball; back-lift high

Fig. 56  On impact, arms straight; bat as parallel as possible; head forwards; roll the wrists to keep the ball down; don't swing too quickly through the ball because this will create a top edge

Fig. 57 Follow through with the head turning towards the ball

# Reverse sweep

Because bowlers have become exceptionally proficient at bowling to their fields, especially in one-day cricket, this shot has taken on a regular role in the first-class game, and can be played by anyone if perfected. A batsman plays within his own limitations; really good players have no limitations!

The reverse sweep is played to a ball of good length, usually outside off-stump, against a bowler defending the leg side.

Play the reverse sweep at your risk. You stand to upset the bowler and the fieldsmen because it has not been accepted yet as part of the game. Good luck . . .

**Fig. 58 (Right)** The batsman has decided to sweep; he has stepped forwards, bat held high; notice that he has picked the bat up and turned the face to cover, as advocated by early MCC coaching books – the difference here is that he has brought the hand forwards slightly

**Fig. 59** After making the decision to reverse sweep, the bottom hand moves quickly on top of and in front of the top hand

**Fig. 60** The shot is completed by the hands hitting down and through the ball, angling it towards and past slip; head down, keep your eye on the ball

# RUNNING BETWEEN THE WICKETS

No-one enjoys being run out. Often mis-understandings are caused by poor technique and a lack of knowledge. There *are* some basic principles.

There are only three calls: 'Wait', 'Yes' and 'No'. What do they mean?

● 'Wait': 'I am not sure, but I will make a final decision. Stay there but be on the alert!'

● 'Yes': 'Run, trust me.'

● 'No': 'I am not moving.'

So, basically, there is nothing to worry about!

## Who calls for what and when?

The simple rules are as follows: the striker calls for all runs that he hits in front of the wicket (and he calls early); the non-striker calls for all runs behind the wicket (and he calls early).

So what can go wrong? The first doubt is cast when the non-caller watches the ball and not his partner. This is called 'ball watching' and is the major cause of confusion. If you follow the principles above, nothing theoretically should go wrong!

## Running more than a single

Calling for more than a single demands new forms of communication. As you pass your partner, make him aware of your thoughts. For example: 'Two there Bob'. Now when you touch down and turn it is your decision because the original caller has now become the non-caller and you are probably running to the danger end. You must respond immediately you are sure that you can make your ground, and at the same time that your partner will also be able to make it. So communicate as you pass on the pitch.

## Running and turning

In order to ensure that you receive the maximum reward for a good shot, follow the next sequence carefully.

● Run the first run quickly, *always.*

● Put the bat in the appropriate hand which allows you to turn facing the ball.

● As you reach the other end, keep low so that you can make yourself longer to cut down the distance you need to run. Remember, only the bat has to cross the line.

● In tight situations, ensure that you slide the bat in at least a yard out from the crease.

● If you are confronted by the striker running on your side of the wicket, the basic principle to follow is that the non-striker runs wider . . .

● . . . especially if the bowler decides to bowl around the wicket.

There are many reasons why you should become what has commonly been termed a 'run thief'. The importance of one run has often been highlighted by one-day results. Good, disciplined running between the wickets is vital.

# BOWLING

I was once asked by the late Colin Page, for many years coach at Kent C.C.C., 'There are two types of bowling. What are they?' I was stumped for an answer. However, to keep you out of your misery I will tell you – fast and slow.

# FAST AND MEDIUM PACE BOWLING

What makes a fast bowler? The majority of great fast bowlers have had one thing in common – suppleness. There are exceptions to this rule. Those who were not so blessed have had to work very hard to maintain it. Certainly of the fast bowlers that I have witnessed, from Trueman to Donald, they have all been extremely loose: very few have had a problem touching their toes (in fact, Donald goes past his toes by 9in (23cm)!). The great West Indian fast bowler Wes Hall once said: 'Man, if you want to bowl fast you must be loose'.

How quick is a fast bowler? Most 'quickies' have at some stage in their careers bowled between 80 and 100 mph. In my experience, most of the top fast bowlers of the recent era have been about the same pace, with one or two able to bowl an exceptionally quick delivery. The two that impressed me for pace were Jeff Thomson of Australia and Michael Holding of the West Indies. But the key to all these quickies' success has been their ability to make the ball move. Two of today's greatest bowlers – Waqar Younis and Wasim Akram – have the ability to swing the ball at great pace.

So, each bowler has his strengths. (For sheer stamina and being able to bowl quickly, Dennis Lillee at his prime would take some beating.) All the greats were supremely fit, supple and strong. High levels of fitness are vital for quick bowlers, indeed for all bowlers. Stretching and training programmes appear in the 'Fitness' chapter, which starts on page 88.

## Grip

As in batting, there is a basic grip for fast and medium pace bowling. This is shown in figs 61 and 62. Notice the first two fingers on either side of the seam (or, if you prefer, *on* the seam), the thumb on the bottom, and the ball resting on the last joint of the fingers, with a small gap in between. This is also the basic seamer's grip. Naturally, grips vary to suit the type of bowler you wish to become. These varieties will be dealt with as we discuss each type of bowling.

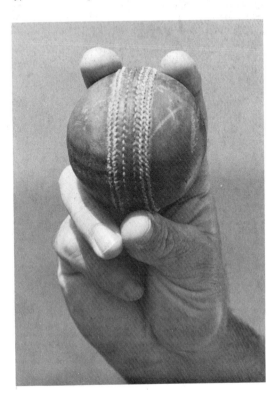

**Fig. 61  Basic grip (from front)**

## Basic action

It sounds as though the bowling action is a highly complicated manoeuvre, and to be fair it is. I believe, however, that it is vital to know what can affect the delivery of the ball, and therefore be able to control it.

One must also remember that the five basic steps occur as one; it takes a good deal of careful scrutiny and use of video equipment to be able to spot and correct mistakes.

Bear in mind too that a number of bowlers have matured physically with a specific action which, when changed, has caused havoc to their bowling. The principles of bowling have to be adjusted to cope with these variations.

**Fig. 62 (Left)** Basic grip (from side): notice the ball resting on the last joint of the fingers, with a small gap visible

**Fig. 63** This position is commonly known as 'the gather'; the front arm extends high (to the edge of the 'coin'); the body turns sideways; back foot is parallel to the crease; the head looks over the front shoulder; the ball in the hand of the bowling arm points down towards the target

**Fig. 64** The completion of the gather, bringing the front knee up and creating the 'rock back' (cocking of a gun) position which is the start of the uncoiling of the spring effect; the bowling arm now extends down towards the bottom of the 'coin'

**Fig. 65**

**Fig. 66**

**Fig. 67**

**Fig. 65** Here the bowler unwinds towards his target; his front foot comes forwards in conjunction with the front arm; the two arms are now virtually parallel to the ground; the front arm initially brings the head forwards and over the top of a braced and straight front leg; some might advocate a slightly bent front knee in order to provide the body with some shock absorption – this is acceptable as long as the front leg then straightens on the instant of delivery

**Fig. 66** The delivery position; note the head level, eyes concentrating on the target (What is the target? A spot on the wicket? The off-stump? The batsman's feet? There is no fixed area; bowlers will have to develop their own preference.); obviously, if you are a slow bowler you will be interested to see if the batsman is going to come down the wicket to you; remember, length will be controlled by your rhythm and head position (head leaning back and you will bowl too full, and head forwards and you will bowl too short)

**Fig. 67** The follow-through; note that the body has made a complete turn (the rear edge of the coin is now facing the target); this is as necessary as the follow-through with any of the batting shots; if the follow-through is not complete, you can be pretty sure that the action does not have enough momentum, and the ball will have been *pushed* towards the target as opposed to having been bowled; for the purpose of the laws, the follow-through has to take the bowler off the pitch; one of the most common faults is that the follow-through starts too soon and the bowler has to adjust his delivery, the ball inevitably going down the leg side

# Run-up

The basic action will only work if the bowler and his run-up have sufficient momentum and rhythm. For example, take a coin and roll it on its side; as it slows down it will start to stall and fall. The precise force exerted on that coin will determine how straight it will run and how long it will stay upright.

Now imagine that the five basic parts of the action resemble a coin in motion. To do this trace your arms in extension around a large imaginary coin. Any stray movement and the coin will fall off to one side or the other and so will your action.

The basic action also relies on timing. The release of the ball in conjunction with the biomechanical movements of the body will determine length and accuracy of delivery.

The run-up varies from bowler to bowler. It must be smooth and rhythmical, which means it must start from the same spot and the feet must repeatedly hit the same areas when running in. There must be no stuttering, and the momentum must be sufficient to drive the action and the ball towards the target accurately.

The run-up is a vital part of the whole action. Just as a long-jumper's approach requires exact measuring, so does a bowler's run-up. Apart from being able to deliver the ball in the correct area, he must not put his front foot over the popping crease or his back foot outside the return crease (*see* figs 68–71).

The often contentious issue with the no ball ruling is that of the raised heel. If, for example, the front foot goes over the line and, on the toes, the heel is in the air but, if grounded, would have cut the line, it is considered to be a fair delivery. It is a brave umpire who calls a no ball, saying that the heel was over the front line while in the air and the ball is being released.

**Fig. 68 Back foot touches the return crease: no ball**

**Fig. 69** Front foot cuts the popping crease:
legal delivery

**Fig. 70** Front foot over the popping crease: no ball

**Fig. 71   Front foot heel on the popping crease: no ball**

## Taking wickets

Having established how to get the ball into the right areas, how do we take wickets? . . . And what are the 'right' areas?

The major wicket-taking deliveries of seamers are balls that deceive the batsman as to where his off-stump is. Terry Alderman was the first bowler that I heard refer to the 'corridor of uncertainty' just outside the off-stump. This area allows a bowler to bring the ball back either in the air or off the seam, teasing the batsman to leave it or to play it. There were few better exponents in recent years of bowling down this corridor than Terry Alderman (there were few better exponents of swinging the ball too).

I intend to touch on two methods whereby a bowler can dismiss batsmen: seam and swing.

## Seam

Seam bowling requires a very high bowling arm and a loose wrist which flicks down the seam of the ball, this motion creating a small area of hard skin on the bowler's index finger. The seam revolves in a backwards motion, creating stability, and allowing the seam to grip on the wicket. The type of wicket that a seam bowler therefore relishes is one that grips, i.e. one usually with plenty of grass, but also a slow, damp wicket. Certain countries favour seam bowlers as opposed to genuinely quick bowlers, English conditions generally favouring the former while the West Indies, with little grass on wickets, favour the latter.

Many seam bowlers will also swing the ball.

# Swing

Essentially, a cricket ball is made from four quarters, and is separated into two halves by a proud seam. The ingredients for swing bowling start with the seam of the ball being used as a rudder. Other ingredients necessary are a good basic action; a subtle difference in grip; a slight difference in the release of the ball; possibly a change in action; and an understanding of the science of the moving cricket ball. Let's deal first with the change of grip.

Fig. 72   Grip for out-swinger

## Out-swinger

The out-swinger grip as depicted in fig. 72 shows the wrist angled in towards the body and cocked backwards, the side of the thumb resting on the seam and the 'rudder' angling towards first slip. To derive maximum effect from the out-swinger the ball must be released fractionally behind the ear (not easy to practise) as it goes past and not too close to the head. But the hand and the body must stay on line and the follow-through must be complete. To enhance the swing the ball must be polished on one side and left rough on the other, the theory being that the shiny side of the ball goes through the air quicker than the dull side. Tactically, the out-swinger aims to get the batsman caught in the slips and gully areas and, if bowled straighter, can trap the batsman LBW. It should be the stock ball of every bowler who wants to succeed in the game.

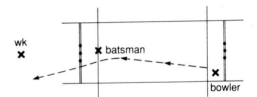

Fig. 73   Path of out-swing

## In-swinger

The in-swinger grip as depicted in fig. 74 shows clearly the seam now angled towards leg slip, and the flat part of the thumb (very important) now resting on the base of the seam – this has the effect of cocking the wrist forwards. The ball now needs to be released in front of the head and the follow-through should be not quite so complete as with the out-swinger. Tactically, the in-swinger is used to tie the batsman down, cramping him for room. Used well, it can cause chaos.

   Many bowlers find this ball easy to bowl because the action does not have to be 'classic'. By trying to bowl a little quicker, the action of

Fig. 74   Grip for in-swinger

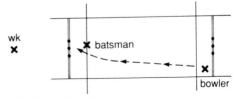

Fig. 75   Path of in-swing

**Fig. 76  Grip for off-cutter: ball pitches and moves to leg side (arrow depicts movement of fingers down side of ball)**

many a young cricketer falls away early, resulting in a preponderance of in-swing bowlers at an early age.

In-swing is also very effective because most cricketers' techniques are not developed to cope with the ball coming in to them; many leave a large 'gate' (gap) between bat and pad – an inexcusable defensive shortcoming.

So, we have dealt with the swinging ball, or have we?

Much has been made of 'reverse swing' and

tampering with the ball, which is illegal. However, in certain countries where the outfields are devoid of grass, the ball becomes scuffed-up very quickly and continual applications of sweat soak into the ball and make one side heavy. Although that side may be the one being polished, the ball may start to 'reverse': use the seam as the rudder by putting the shiny side the way you want to swing the ball – it will react differently and confuse those batsmen who look for the shine or difference in

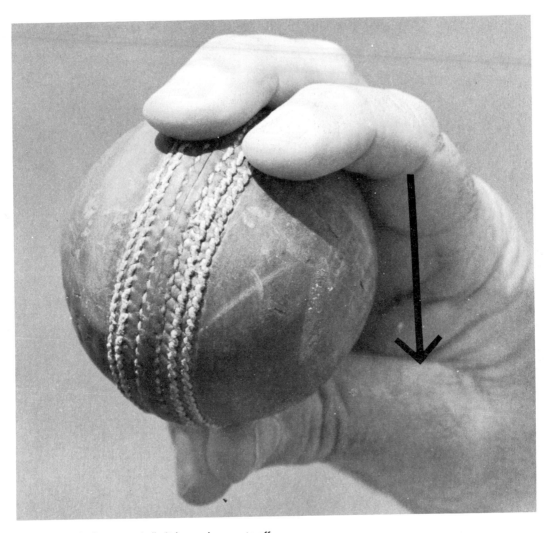

**Fig. 77  Grip for leg-cutter: ball pitches and moves to off side (arrow depicts movement of fingers down side of ball)**

colour. The scratching of the ball increases the drag and, bowled at top speeds, gives it a sharp and late swing, mainly into the bat.

For the majority of club and schoolboy cricketers, games do not last long enough for these techniques to be developed. But there is no doubt that the swinging ball bowled accurately is a devastating weapon.

For medium pace bowlers who struggle to swing the ball (and there are times when the conditions do not help swing bowlers) there is a call for different methods.

## Cut

For a swing or seam bowler to have an effect, he will have to learn to 'cut' the ball. He does this employing the same basic action and grips, but altering the seam on the ball to more of an acute angle and pulling his fingers down the side of the ball, making it rotate sufficiently to grip and move after it pitches. (This is also one way of bowling an effective slower ball: the same action is employed but the hand comes down the side of the ball, automatically slowing it down.

# SLOW BOWLING

Slow bowling is an art in itself, but it is based on exactly the same principles as all bowling, with one major difference . . .

## Finger-spin

In order to impart finger-spin or orthodox spin on the ball, e.g. off-spin or left-arm orthodox, the body has to swivel and this can only be done by landing on the toes, the bowling arm cutting across the body. This, allied to vigorous finger-spin, creates maximum turn. The position of the arm, again, must be at a low angle from the head: all the great spinners have had reasonably 'low' arms.

The grips for the orthodox finger-spinner are shown in figs 78–80.

Tactically, bowling spin needs patience and an unruffled constitution when being hit for the odd six. The art requires supreme accuracy because any lapse in length can be punished unmercifully.

At the top level, changes of pace have to come from a fairly brisk stock ball in order to try and discourage batsmen from using their feet, allowing you the luxury of having fieldsmen around them, putting them under pressure so that they feel that they have to play differently.

Once you have achieved this you will have started to master the art of spin bowling. Another major factor for a spinner to develop is 'loop'. If you have studied how a tennis ball dips after a fierce top-spin shot, you will understand this phenomenon. Loop is created by imparting 'real' spin, not 'gentle' spin (i.e. merely 'rolling' the ball out), allied to a fast bowling arm action and a slow front arm action.

World class spin bowlers will have perfected

**Fig. 78  Spread the first and second fingers on to the seam of the ball, ensuring that the major pressure is exerted on the first finger**

this. It is a real joy to play against because it really tests the batsman's ability to pick length.

Spinners tend to mature later in their careers since it takes a great deal of bowling to gain the necessary accuracy, and confidence is often dented by being hit hard early in a career. Stick at it; it can be really rewarding.

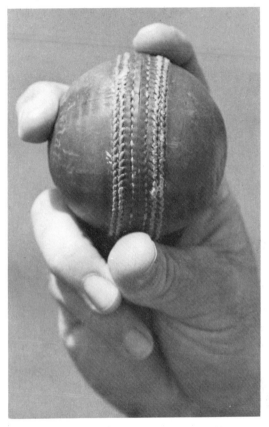

Fig. 79 Fold the hand down behind the ball, bending the fingers; for smaller hands the pressure must be comfortable because the force exerted by the first finger creates the required spin; then cock the wrist in towards the body during the run-up and the early part of the action, and only when you release the ball do you 'open the door' and flick the forefinger out. The right-armer's off-spinner is designed to bowl batsmen out through the gate, or caught in the leg trap. The variation is to beat the batsman on the other side of the bat by bowling what is commonly called a 'floater' as in fig. 80

Fig. 80 Using a spread-finger grip to fool the batsman, hold the ball so that the first finger runs down the seam; the thumb adopts a sideways position as in the out-swinger; instead of spinning the ball it comes off the one finger and floats away from the batsman, who you are hoping is playing for the turn – you may then have a chance of having him caught behind, or at slip, or even stumped if he has come down the wicket at you. For the left-arm orthodox bowler who is turning the ball away from the bat, the floater may well trap the batsman LBW or have him caught at bat-pad playing for the turn. What is the common denominator for both types of bowler is that he must try to go past both edges of the bat

## Wrist-spin

A leg-spinner is a rare breed. It is a skill that takes years of hard graft and devotion in order to master it. A left-arm bowler's over-the-wrist delivery is called a 'chinaman', a ball that is almost extinct in first-class cricket.

The googly is the alternative ball if you remember that we are trying to go past both edges of the bat. Among other alternatives are the top-spinner, the flipper and the quicker ball.

These variations, plus the basic leg-spinner, have to be practised a great deal in order to obtain the necessary accuracy: accuracy is almost as important as spinning the ball.

The grip for wrist-spinning does not rely on the pressure points of the fingers as much as orthodox spinning, but relies on a very supple wrist. The grip starts with the first and third fingers running down the seam of the ball, with the second finger resting on top. Fold the hand down behind the ball until the thumb is running parallel to the seam (*see* fig. 81). Cock the wrist down and away from the body. As the arm swings over in the bowling action, the wrist flicks open as if you are opening a door anti-clockwise. It is important to keep the bowling arm very high when delivering the ball: this will create the natural in-drift and dip that can be enhanced even more if bowling into the wind. The natural variation is the googly, depicted in figs 82 and 83.

Bowling is the tough part of cricket. While batting is glamorous, a bowler can bowl brilliantly all day without taking a wicket. It takes great strength of character, fitness, stamina and skill to be a bowler. Few matches are won without the opposition being bowled out (except in the one-day game).

**Fig. 81  Grip for wrist-spinning**

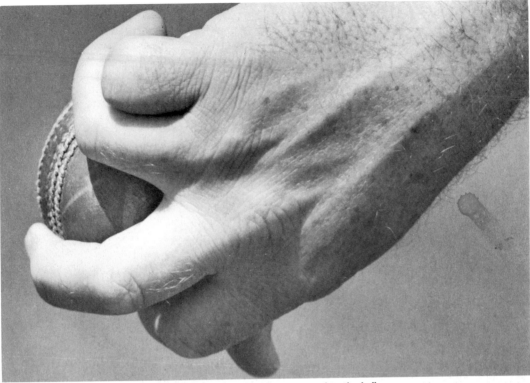

Fig. 82   The back of the hand faces the batsman at delivery, as opposed to the ball

Fig. 83   The position of the seam as it comes out of the hand; it turns in towards the batsman with a similar action as the leg-spinner. Bearing in mind just how quickly the arm comes over, you can see how difficult it can be for the batsman to pick which way the ball is going to turn. This naturally causes mistakes and leads to a wicket

# FIELDING

One-day cricket has made the biggest single contribution to the improvement of fielding in the game. Techniques today are honed to a very high level. However, 'Catches still win matches': while a great fielder may be able to save 20 runs in the field, one dropped catch can cost the match . . .

## Catching

### Slip catching

Fig. 84  Knees bent, eyes level, hands ready – the perfect position for the slip fielder. The knees are bent so that the slip catch can be caught without having to bend further; this would cause the head to go down, taking the eyes off the line of the ball. The position also allows the fielder to dive as would a soccer goalkeeper and, as importantly, to jump for the high slip catch. (At this point always remember it is easier to go up than down.) At slip it is vital to keep the head still until you have had a chance to judge the catch, which quite often comes very quickly and the reaction time is very small. Keeping the head still will make it much easier

**Fig. 85** When a straightforward slip catch comes your way, it is still important to have the correct technique. Hands must point down and be 'soft', with a little 'give'. If they start too close to the body, the jarring effect of the hands on the body can knock the ball out

Fig. 86 Taking the ball to the right or left also requires technical competence. The fingers must point out away from the body and you must create a large catching area by keeping the fingers spread wide. When catching it is important to let the hands 'give' on the line of the ball, at the same time having 'soft' hands so that the force of the ball closes them. The head moves as close to the line as is possible, which helps the weight-transfer turn the hips out of the way to allow ease of movement

Fig. 87 The ball is wider and it is only possible to catch with one hand

Fig. 88   In this case it is dropping short so the fielder, having taken the ball, has started to roll inwards to keep the ball off the ground (If it had gone quickly, he would have to roll backwards.)

Fig. 89   The importance of the roll is to cushion the jar and yet many fielders land on the elbow, which causes the hand to fly open and the ball to escape

## High Catching

Catching the high ball requires good judgement, concentration and courage. The following principles should be followed.

Firstly, attempt to judge where the ball will land; then get to that area as fast as your legs will carry you, to allow you to make final adjustments. Keep the head still and the hands high. As you are about to catch the ball, spread the fingers wide, making as large a surface as possible for the ball to hit (*see* fig. 90).

### English method

**Fig. 90** Note the position of the hands held high; use the tips of the fingers as a guide to the flight of the ball; knees slightly bent, body as relaxed as possible (don't tense up)

Fig. 91 'Giving' with the ball is important, but only to chest height; keep your eyes on the ball

## Australian method

The majority of high catches in the UK are made easier by cloud cover. In countries which tend to have beautiful blue skies, it is more useful to use the Australian method.

**Fig. 92  Hands held high; palms are now facing the ball; your view of the ball is helped by the fingers, spread wide**

# Ground fielding

Speed across the ground is vital when practising getting to the ball.

**Fig. 93  The 'give' after catching the ball must be reduced; bend the elbows and take the ball down to your chest**

**Fig. 94 'Long barrier' position**

## Defensive fielding

There are occasions when the ball is hit at the fieldsman with great power or on a bumpy outfield. In both these cases it is important to adopt the 'long barrier' position as in fig. 94. Here you will notice that the fielder is right-handed, which means he must get down on his left knee. His first priority is to get the right foot at right angles to the path of the ball. He then gets down on his left knee, tucking it against the heel of the right foot. The hand collects the ball under the eyes and with the right foot as the second line of defence. In fig. 95 the fielder has jumped up off his right foot. He is sideways-on, in the perfect position to throw the ball in quickly.

**Fig. 95**

## Attacking the ball

Fig. 96 Balance is very important. As you approach the ball make sure that you are able to get the correct foot to the ball. Get sideways-on. The right foot acts as the second line of defence

Fig. 97 The alternative is the one-handed pick-up. The dangers of this pick-up are obvious, but speed is necessary to induce run outs. Keeping low and bending the knees are key factors, as well as superb timing. On bumpy outfields it is safer to use the previous method

Fig. 98 Because the fielder has kept sideways-on, he is in a perfect position to get up, aim with his left arm . . .

Fig. 99 . . . and follow through, keeping the head going towards the target

# Chasing the ball and throwing on the turn

When chasing the ball it is vital for the bowler's and the team's confidence that the chase is hard. Depending on which is your throwing arm, make sure that you keep the ball on that side of the body if you are going to pick up and throw on the turn.

Fig. 100   The fielder picks the ball up by his right foot

Fig. 101   Staying low and still moving away from the wicket, the fielder takes his weight on to his left foot from which he will jump

Fig. 102   The jump and turn created by the head turning and the front arm aiming

Fig. 103   As both feet leave the ground the throw commences; a brilliant piece of fielding

**Fig. 100**

**Fig. 101**

**Fig. 102**

**Fig. 103**

Arguably quicker is the latest method – the 'slide-save and throw'.

The slide method can only really be used on a lush grass surface.

Whatever technique you employ, you cannot practise fielding enough, particularly if you have pretensions to play at the top level. If you are only a batsman, make yourself into a top-class fielder too.

Fig. 105 The momentum will stand him up very quickly, already aimed

Fig. 104 The fielder this time has kept the ball on his left side. He has slid on to his left side and knee, steadying himself with his left arm. As he picks up the ball he digs his right foot into the ground and pushes up with the left arm

# Fielding practice

During the season, set yourself certain goals in your fielding ability:

● to have confidence in your ability to pick up the ball cleanly
● to throw the ball in accurately from all distances and positions
● to catch almost anything that is offered
● to never mis-field a ball.

Use the following practices to highlight the individual skills and help you achieve these goals.

---

**Slip cordon**
(1) 'Nicks' off edge of bat (×3 players)
(2) Left & right hand catching
(3) Diving & rolling technique (use mat)
(4) High one-handers
(5) Head-high two-handers
(6) Awkward height catching

---

**Silly point**
(1) Correct positioning
(2) Watching area
(3) Staying down for as long as possible
(4) Avoidance technique, but staying alert for possible rebounds
(5) Positive reactions to 'Catch it!' calls
(6) Importance of position to exert pressure

---

**Fig. 106   The fielder is in a perfect position to get the ball in**

## Inner ring

*Defence*
(1) Dealing with hard hits while walking in from crouched position
(2) Stopping one-handed
(3) Long barrier; body blocking

*Attack*
(1) Pick up and throw on the run in one movement (overarm and underarm)
(2) Changing direction of throw on call 'Bowler!' or 'Keeper!'
(3) Attacking the stumps
(4) Learning to choose the correct option (Fielder calls from opposite side as he has the best view of the action.)
(5) Throwing on the turn (include 'dummy')
(6) Chasing and sliding to knock ball back from boundary; knocking ball back so that it is easy to collect
(7) Catching on the run (forwards, backwards, left & right)
(8) Catching on the turn (noise of bat activates movement of fielder)

## Short leg (forward & backward)
(1) Proper technique (watch ball or front pad)
(2) Catching within reach: reaction work
(3) Simulated catching (three in a group)
(4) Diving & rolling (forwards & to side)
(5) Avoiding injury (cushioning)
(6) Acting as 'keeper for quick run out to cover
(7) Feet position
(8) Staying down
(9) Catching the fended-down bouncer

## Outer ring
(1) Making ground quickly to the ball, timing foot movements to coincide with the best pick-up and throwing position
(2) Diving or sliding to prevent boundary
(3) Judgement of high catches using rope as a guide
(4) Developing the one-bounce throw to gain that extra yard
(5) Practising getting the ball into the air early to prevent the chance of another run

## Gully
(1) Practise technique – balls slashed at gully from a thrower
(2) Diving left & right
(3) Rolling and reaction movements

These are just a few games that will enhance a team's performance in the field. Remember, practise with discipline.

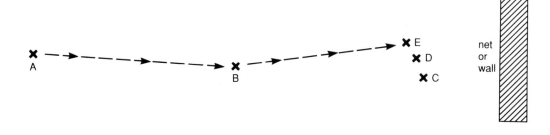

**Fig. 107** Slip fielding (A=thrower; B=batsman; C, D, E=catchers): A throws the ball to B, hard and flat at about waist height; B uses the bat to nick the ball off the face to the three fielders (Groups of five are ideal.)

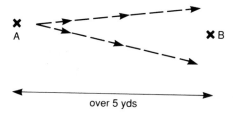

**Fig. 108** Slip fielding: reaction – A throws the ball over 5 yds to B; B starts with his back turned; A says 'Now!' fractionally before he throws

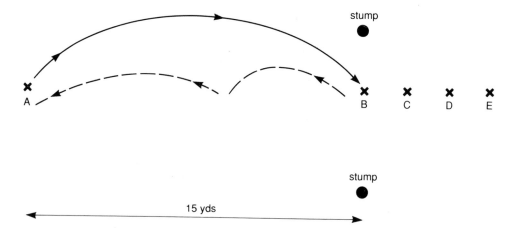

**Fig. 109** Cover catching (A=hitter; B, C, D and E=fielders): A hits the ball in turn to the fielders, who line up between two stumps; having caught the ball, the fielders lob the ball on one bounce back to A; A gets one point every time the catchers drop the ball, but he loses one point if he hits the ball wide of the stumps. As a variation, add a third stump and a wicket-keeper next to A; the fielders throw the ball in hard to the 'keeper

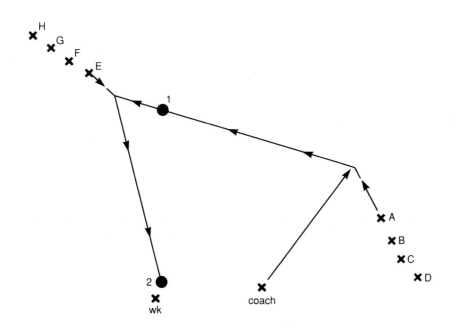

**Fig. 110** Throwing for run outs: the coach rolls the ball along the ground for A to run on to; A picks up the ball on the run and shies at stump 1; fielder E backs up the throw and throws the ball to the wicket-keeper at stump 2; having thrown, each fielder runs around and joins the end of the opposite team

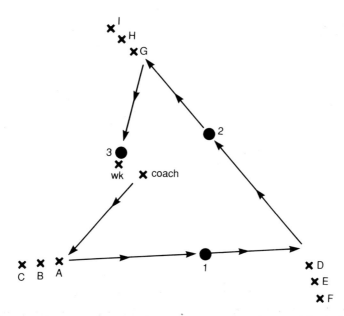

**Fig. 111** Throwing for run outs (advanced): the coach rolls the ball to fielder A; A under-arms the ball to stump 1; fielder D collects the ball and shies at stump 2; fielder G backs up this throw and throws to the wicket-keeper at stump 3; after throwing, each fielder runs to join the next group

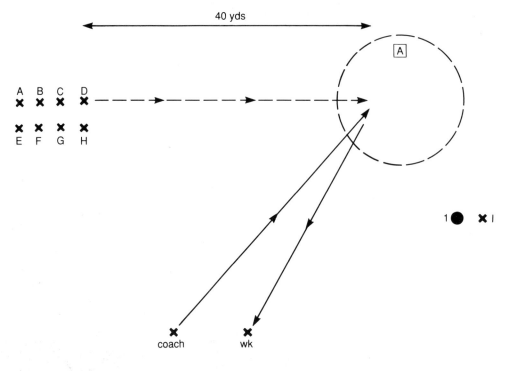

**Fig. 112** Running and throwing: the coach hits the ball to area A; fielder D runs (about 40 yds) to collect the ball and throws to the wicket-keeper; in the meantime, batsmen I and J attempt to run two runs between stumps 1 and 2

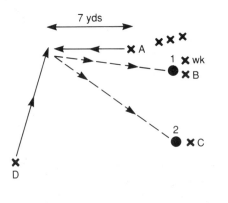

**Fig. 113** Running and throwing: fielder D hits the ball approximately 7 yds to the right hand of fielder A; as he hits the ball, fielders B and C attempt to run a single between stumps 1 and 2; fielder F calls to fielder A which end he should throw to, and backs up the throw if at stump 2; the wicket-keeper backs up if the throw is at stump 1; fielders F and A change places, and so on

# WICKET-KEEPING

The wicket-keeper plays one of the most vital roles on the cricket field. Apart from the obvious fact that every delivery is sent in his direction, he has to lead by example; every throw, good or bad, he has to tidy up; he has to encourage the bowler, answering questions like 'Am I hitting the gloves hard?', 'What is my front arm like?', 'Is the ball doing anything?', and so on; he has to run to his stumps for every return, and chase round the batsman to collect defensive prods. He is the life and soul of the

party: even if he drops a catch or misses a stumping his enthusiasm must never waver!

Want the job? First you will need the right equipment. Modern wicket-keeping pads are small and very light. Gloves are vital. Comfort is a priority: they must feel as though they are part of the hand. Inners should ideally be made of chamois. Wear more than one pair if the ball starts to bruise the hands, or if you are playing a lot of cricket, or when 'keeping to really fast bowlers. The joints of each finger should be

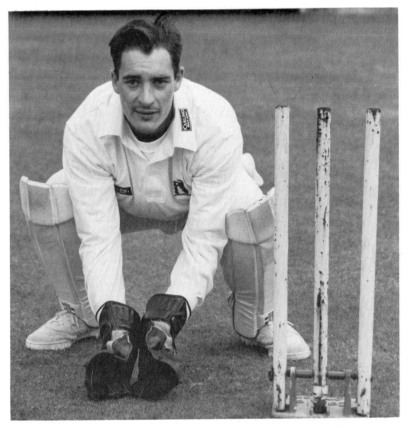

**Fig. 114   The feet are just over shoulder-width apart; left foot covering the off-stump; hands placed forwards; arms relaxed; head and eyes level. The alternative (not recommended) is to have the hands start either side of the feet, with the feet closer together. The drawback to this technique is that the hands have to be brought back together before the ball is taken**

taped up to offer support because it is very easy to dislocate or break a finger if you catch the ball awkwardly. Finally, you will need an abdominal protector.

Having kitted yourself out properly, remember one vital piece of information: expect every ball to come to you, whether you're standing up or back.

The technique of wicket-keeping has advanced like the equipment. We will deal only with the basic requirements.

## Stances

Comfort is again a prerequisite. Study the two photographs.

**Fig. 115  The wicket-keeper has moved down the leg side to take the ball. Notice that the right foot has remained within striking distance of the stumps for a possible leg-side stumping. What is crucial here, and applies to both sides of the wicket, is the position of the hands: they have remained low, waiting for the ball to bounce, and then they rise with the ball**

**Fig. 116  The hands are just taking the ball, and you can see the difference in height. Notice that the fingers remain pointing down. If the hands and fingers come up too soon, a fumble will be the inevitable result**

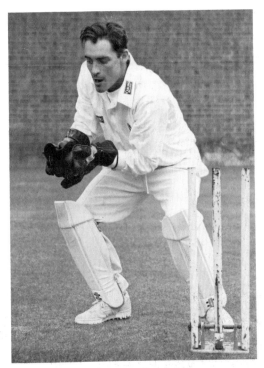

Fig. 117    The correct position of the fingers in taking the ball

Fig. 118    Difficulties often arise when the ball bounces. Here you can see that the 'keeper has turned his right hip out of the way, making room for the hands to work. One of the basic errors that young 'keepers make is trying to get the body behind the ball. It is very difficult when the ball moves or swings, bounces or turns, to move the hands because the body is in the way. Wicket-keepers must use their hands

Fig. 119    The 'keeper has dived to his right and spread himself so that his arm is at full stretch. Diving and rolling were covered in the slip fielding section on pages 62–5

**Fig. 120** Get the coach or a team-mate to throw the ball at you under-arm so that you can work on all aspects of taking the ball

**Fig. 121** Take the ball one-handed, making sure that the fingers point out and that the head takes the weight across to the line of the ball. Ensure that the hands keep on the line of the ball

Being able to stand back to take outside edges which keep low is very important because often the wicket-keeper is on his own.

Practise taking the ball behind a batsman. Here you will need two colleagues: a bowler or thrower, throwing the ball to your instructions; and a batsman deliberately missing the ball.

By throwing a tennis ball against a wall, with no gloves, you can simulate the same effect: the tennis ball will encourage you to take the ball by the nature of its design and composition.

Concentrate, be fit, and, above all, be enthusiastic!

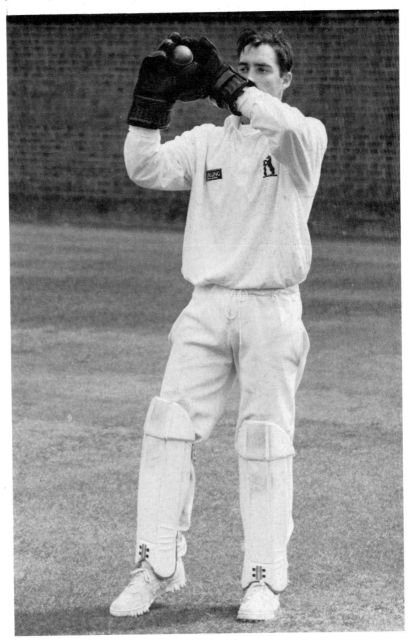

Fig. 122 When taking the ball above or level with your head, use your strongest hand to catch the ball, supporting it with the other hand

# CAPTAINCY

What makes a good captain?

● **Leadership qualities.** A captain must have the ability to lead his side by performance and thereby gain the respect of his players. He must not shirk any of the 'dirty' duties.

● **Man-management skills.** He must know what makes each member of his team tick so that he can motivate them to perform to the best of their ability.

● **Sound tactical skills.** He must know when to attack and when to defend. He must have complete control of field placings and be able to ascertain batsmen's weaknesses and exploit them.

● **Knowledge of the laws and competitions.** Often a certain law or a change in competition rules can have a profound effect on the game. The captain must be completely clued-up so that he can make the correct decisions.

● **Discipline.** There are times when a captain has to crack the whip if a player argues with an umpire. He must ensure that the game is conducted in the right spirit.

● **Compassion.** Occasionally players fail and have to be dropped. The captain must be able to handle these and other problems with diplomacy.

● **Ruthlessness.** When he has a side on the run, he must 'go for the jugular', and not let the opposition off the hook.

● **Administrative capabilities.** A captain has

certain roles, depending on the club. He must make sure that he:
(a) puts up the team sheet on the notice-board
(b) ensures that tea and lunch are organised
(c) arranges the travelling for away games
(d) on match days: assesses the wicket; tosses with the opposing captain; decides on whether to bat or bowl; posts the batting order; motivates the team; tells them what his initial ideas are and who is going to open the bowling.

Captaincy is a heavy responsibility and not for the faint-hearted.

## Field placing

Field placing in the modern game has become a much more methodical element of captaincy. Not only should the captain know how and when to manipulate his fielders, the fielders themselves must realise the job expected of them in their particular positions. One-day cricket has created far more defensive-orientated fields due to the number and range of shots that batsmen are prepared to play (e.g. the reverse sweep).

The various positions on the field (*see* figs 123–130) make cricket a game of outdoor chess. Bowlers must know the difference between attack and defence, and be able to cope with them by varying their length. Fielders must realise what the bowler is trying to do to each batsman, and be awake to the minutest variation designed to exert pressure on the batsman.

Fielding is the simplest criteria for measuring the improvement in the game's standards.

I would like to think that each person studying these field placings would have his own ideas and variations and adapt them to the batsman, the conditions and the state of the game.

As a captain, it is important to run the game from a prominent position, i.e. slip, mid-wicket or mid-off (but remember that there is a tendency to stand too close to the bat while fielding at mid-off).

Reduce the distance that fielders have to move from over to over where possible, but more importantly put the specialist fielders in their rightful positions and don't move them just because they make a mistake. Last but not least, remember that you cannot set a field for a bad ball!

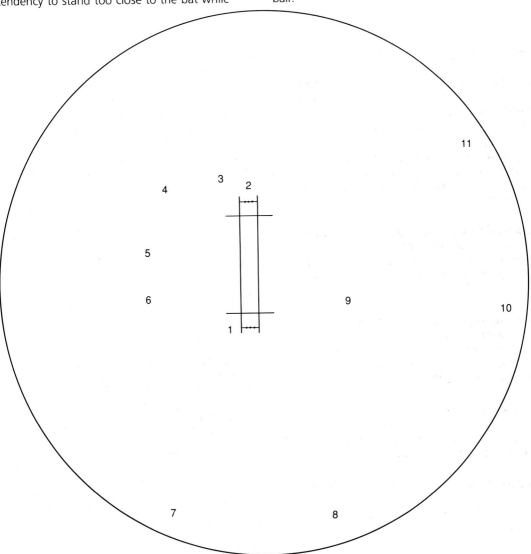

**Fig. 123 Defensive field for leg-spin/googly bowler. Key: 1 bowler; 2 wicket-keeper; 3 slip; 4 backward point; 5 cover; 6 extra cover; 7 deep mid-off; 8 deep mid-on; 9 mid-wicket (straight); 10 deep mid-wicket; 11 deep backward square leg. The slip is optional: he could be placed as an extra man on the leg side, or indeed on the** off side. Depending which side the bowler is attempting to attack, the backward point could go finer for the late cut: by moving him squarer you might induce the batsman to play across the line and edge it in attempting to work the ball fine

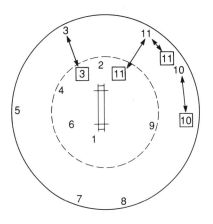

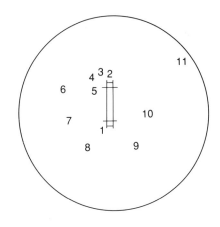

**Fig. 124  Defensive field (one-day onslaught!) to a seamer.** Key: 1 bowler; 2 wicket-keeper; 3 third man; 4 backward point; 5 deep cover ('sweeper'); 6 extra cover (straight); 7 deep mid-off; 8 deep mid-on; 9 mid-wicket (straight); 10 long leg; 11 fine leg. The bowler must bowl full-length yorkers, low full tosses and long half-volleys so that orthodox batsmen are forced to hit the ball straight. The extra cover and the straight mid-wicket would save the single, and a straight hit should only get one run. If you need to keep four men in the circle, bring either the third man or the fine leg into the ring. To prevent the slog over mid-wicket, the fine leg may have to move to long leg, moving the long leg to deep mid-wicket

**Fig. 125  Left-arm orthodox slow bowling on a turning wicket.** Key: 1 bowler; 2 wicket-keeper; 3 first slip; 4 second slip; 5 silly point; 6 point or backward point; 7 extra cover; 8 mid-off; 9 mid-on; 10 mid-wicket; 11 deep backward square leg. Most batsmen will attempt to play off the back foot. Therefore, the backward point, extra cover and mid-off need to be adjusted according to the batsman's technique. The mid-wicket needs to be very straight in order to encourage the batsman to play across the ball, so inducing a top edge

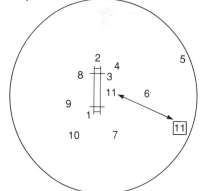

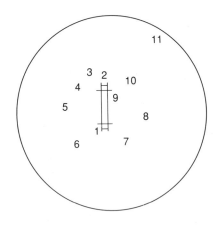

**Fig. 126  Off-spin bowling on a turning wicket.** Key: 1 bowler; 2 wicket-keeper; 3 bat-pad; 4 backward short leg; 5 deep backward square leg; 6 mid-wicket; 7 mid-on; 8 silly point; 9 extra cover; 10 mid-off, 11 silly mid-wicket or deep mid-wicket. The extra cover must be straight, encouraging the batsman to hit the ball square, opening his gate; also, the ball is more likely to go straight because of the turn. This also allows the mid-off to go slightly deeper. Depending on the batsman's tactics, the mid-wicket would have to be either close in or deep. On occasion, the deep backward square leg could be brought in to encourage the batsman to sweep, so inducing a top edge

**Fig. 127  In-swing bowling (medium fast) to a right-handed batsman.** Key: 1 bowler; 2 wicket-keeper; 3 slip; 4 gully; 5 cover; 6 mid-off; 7 mid-on; 8 mid-wicket; 9 bat-pad; 10 backward short leg; 11 fine leg. Since only two fielders are permitted behind square on the leg side, it may be necessary, in extreme conditions, to bring up fine leg to leg slip. The gully may seem superfluous: however, occasionally the straight ball can loop up off an outside edge, depending on the pace of the pitch

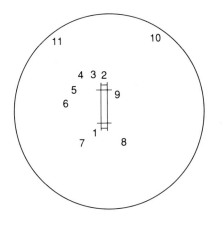

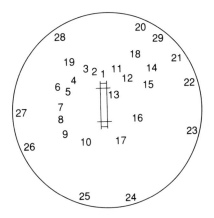

Fig. 128 Out-swing bowling (medium fast) to a right-handed batsman. Key: 1 bowler; 2 wicket-keeper; 3 first slip; 4 second slip; 5 gully; 6 cover point; 7 mid-off; 8 mid-on; 9 bat-pad; 10 fine leg; 11 third man. This is the basic attacking field. If needed, the third man could join the slip cordon. The bat-pad position is there to pick up the inside edge on to the pad square of the wicket, often a result of combating out-swing by playing outside the line of the ball

Fig. 129 General fielding positions (right-arm bowler, right-handed batsman). Key: 1 wicket-keeper; 2 first slip; 3 second slip; 4 gully; 5 point; 6 backward point; 7 cover point; 8 cover; 9 extra cover; 10 mid-off; 11 leg slip; 12 leg gully or backward short leg; 13 bat-pad; 14 backward square leg; 15 square leg; 16 mid-wicket; 17 mid-on; 18 short fine leg; 19 short third man; 20 fine leg; 21 deep backward square leg; 22 deep square leg; 23 deep mid-wicket; 24 long-on; 25 long-off; 26 deep extra cover; 27 deep cover point ('sweeper'); 28 third man; 29 long leg

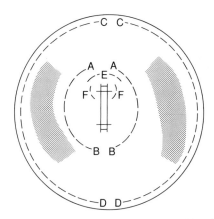

Fig. 130 General criteria for placement of fielders (all types of bowling). Key: A-B inner ring; C-D outer ring; E slip cordon; F short square bat-pad positions; shaded area – no man's land. Fielders in the inner ring save one run. Fielders in the outer ring save four runs. Fielders in the slip cordon are in catching positions for balls off the edge of the bat. Fielders in the short square bat-pad positions are responsible for catching defensive bat-pad shots

# FITNESS

Good players are skilful; the *best* players are also mentally tough and physically fit.

Fitness for cricket has become over the last 20 years a much studied and much maligned subject: much maligned by those who scoff at the antics of today's cricketers; much studied because the correct formula has yet to be reached. The many doubters cite the continual injury problems of many modern players, backing their point up by referring to bowlers who used to bowl over 1000 overs in a season, without ever breaking down. The truth is that today's top bowlers have to bowl as many overs, but they do so in four different competitions, of which three are very intense and stressful (i.e. the one-day format).

So we have to ask: 'Have we kept pace with the issue?'. The answer in my opinion is 'No'; we still have a long way to go. There is a fine line between fatigue and fitness.

Why does a player need to be fit to play cricket?

● Being fit allows you to maintain your skill level for longer periods during the duration of play.

● At practice you can improve your skill level because your fitness means that the quality of practice will not deteriorate.

● Physical fitness can help you resist injury and the onset of fatigue, giving you an added advantage.

● A fit player's career will theoretically last longer. (Though there are exceptions to every rule!)

● Physical fitness can enhance the mental strength of batsman, bowler and fielder.

● If you do not believe in the advantages of being fit, tell me the advantages of being unfit.

Before you read on, you would be wise to answer the following mini-questionnaire. Be honest with yourself about your goals and your motivations.

● Are you satisfied with your current level of fitness?
● Are you strong enough?
● Are you flexible enough?
● Are you working on the specific physical requirements of your particular game?
● Are you prepared to devote more time to improving your fitness?
● In an analysis of your game, in what areas are you most effective? Is this a reflection of your fitness?
● Do you record your performances in each game or analyse how you felt?
● When you train, do you work hard and with enthusiasm, or do you merely go through the motions?

## Training principles

There are eight fundamental principles that a cricketer should consider in connection with his fitness training.

### Quality, not quantity

This principle relates mainly to bowlers. Medium pace bowlers may tend to work in the nets for approximately an hour off a shortened run. It would be more beneficial to bowl at 'match intensity' for several overs, take a rest period and then resume with another intense spell: in other words, to simulate match conditions.

## Progressive overload

The principle of progressive overload lays down that players need to experience more physical stress in training than they do in a game. It applies particularly to pre-season training, but can also play a role throughout the playing season.

Examples of progressive overload training would be batsmen running four or five runs (not one, two or three, as is most usual in games), bowlers jogging back to their mark (not walking) and fielders fielding, returning and chasing another ball immediately afterwards, for up to ten repetitions.

## Specificity

Essentially, cricket training and practice takes place largely in the nets. However, in the nets many factors differ from those in a game. For example, bowlers do not have an opportunity to bowl to a specific field; batsmen are less concerned about hitting the ball loosely in the air; batsmen do not have to consider running between wickets. Practices should be devised to include match-type conditions.

## Regularity

At the game's highest levels, it is very important to train for superior fitness to play, not to play as a means of keeping fit. Daily skills practice and fitness training every other day should be the target of all players.

## Variety

It is not always easy to maintain motivation to practise and train. Varying the activities, the venue, the group leader or instructor will help. Otherwise, it is all too easy to merely go through the motions.

## Individualism

While it is important to have group activities and for all players to be involved, so that motivation can be enhanced through competition between players, it is also important for each player to have his own programme catered to his particular needs. This will vary according to his principal role as a batsman or bowler, his strength levels, his flexibility and his endurance capacity.

## Warm-up and warm down

**Fig. 131   Arm and shoulder stretch**

**Fig. 132 (Right)   Shoulder stretch for the bowling and throwing muscles**

**Fig. 133   Back and abdominal stretch**

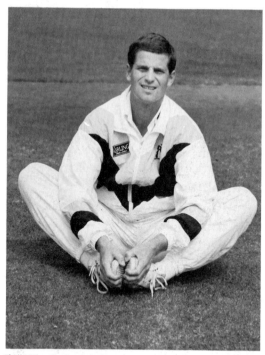

**Fig. 134   Hamstring stretch**

**Fig. 135   Groin stretch**

**Figs 136 and 137   Side bend stretch**

**Fig. 138    Thigh stretch**

**Fig. 139    Buttock stretch**

**Fig. 140    Calf and Achilles stretch**

Too many players have too many injuries. It seems to be readily accepted that frequent injuries are all part of the game. While every team has players who invariably seem to be 'injured', whether they are or not, injury can be avoided to a great extent by running for 15 minutes, stretching and then conducting a skills warm-up. At the end of a training or practice session, repeat the jog for ten minutes, and stretch again for five minutes.

It is absolutely vital for a cricketer to follow a set routine of stretching exercises. This will loosen the body before a game and prevent stiffness and other aches and pains during and after a game. Hold each stretch for a minimum of 20 seconds, then release the stretch slowly. Repeat each stretch at least twice to gain maximum benefit.

## Evaluation

Measuring and evaluating your progress will help you to stay motivated and keeps you in touch with your performances. Apart from the conventional fitness elements, more specific activities can be included. A 20-run 'marathon' with pads and a bat could replace a straightforward 400 m sprint, for instance.

The various programmes outlined in the tables at the end of this chapter have been designed specifically for professional cricketers. However, the principles on which they are based apply to all cricketers, whatever their level of performance.

## Aerobic and anaerobic fitness

Aerobic activity simply means training within one's oxygen range, i.e. a gentle run of 3–4 km: training over a long period, say 30 minutes, but not to the extent that one is breathless.

Anaerobic activity means exactly the opposite, e.g. running for extended periods where the oxygen state is so critical that one has to slow down. Try a sprint of 400 m and repeat it six to 12 times: then you will understand the difference between aerobic and anaerobic.

# Power and strength training

Power and strength training using weights is terribly important to a cricketer because it can lessen the risks of injury and quicken rehabilitation if an injury has occurred.

## Pre-season strength programme

This first programme is designed to *build* more strength. Start it four to six weeks before the start of the season. (This is also the time to incorporate cricket-specific exercises into the gym routine or out in the field.) Get your body ready for playing cricket again.

| Exercises | Sets | Reps |
|---|---|---|
| (1) Sit-ups | 2 | 20–50 per set |
| (or leg raises | 2 | 20–50 (each leg) |
| or trunk rotations) | 1 | 30 |
| (2) Full squats | 4 | 12, 10, 8, 6 |
| (or leg raises | 2 | 15, 15 |
| or hamstring curls | 2 | 15, 15 |
| or lunge/split squats) | 2 | 10, 8 |
| (3) Lateral raises | 4 | 12, 10, 8, 6 |
| (4) Rowing | 4 | 12, 10, 8, 6 |
| (5) Shoulder presses | 4 | 12, 10, 8, 6 |
| (6) Back lifts (using roman chair) | 2 | max.15 (then add weight) |
| (7) Tricep pull downs | 4 | 12, 10, 8, 6 |
| (or tricep thrusts) | 2 | max.12 (then add weight) |
| (8) Bicep curls | 4 | 12, 10, 8, 6 |
| (or wrist curls | 2–3 | 12, 10, (8) (each wrist) |
| or reverse wrist curls) | 2–3 | 12, 10, (8) (each wrist) |

## In-season strength programme

This programme is designed to *maintain* strength levels. Abdominal, rotational and light weight work are essential parts of the in-season schedule. Bowlers in particular should concentrate on light weight shoulder work, i.e. deltoid exercises.

| Exercises | Sets | Reps |
|---|---|---|
| (1) Sit-ups | 1 | 20–50 per set |
| (or dead man's lifts) | 1 | 15–20 |
| (2) Squat thrusts | 2 | 10, 8 |
| (or step-ups) | 1–2 | 10–15 (each leg) |
| (3) Bench presses (light) | 2 | 10, 8 |
| (or pull-ups) | 2 | 10, 10 |
| (4) Lateral pull-downs | 2 | 10, 8 |
| (5) Wrist curls | 2 | 12, 10 (each wrist) |
| (6) Reverse wrist curls | 2 | 12, 10 (each wrist) |

## Off-season strength programme

This programme is designed to strengthen and balance all the major muscle groups of the body. Consult your coach about varying the exercises in the programme to strengthen particular muscular weaknesses and/or correct muscle imbalance.

| Exercises | Sets | Reps |
|---|---|---|
| (1) Sit-ups | 2 | 15–25 per set |
| (or leg raises | 2 | 15–25 |
| or trunk rotations) | 1 | 15–30 |
| (2) Leg raises | 3 | 12, 10, 8 |
| (3) Hamstring curls | 3 | 12, 10, 8 |
| (or squats | 3 | 12, 10, 10 |
| or groin flexes | 2–3 | 12 (each leg) |
| or hip flexes) | 2–3 | 12 (each leg) |
| (4) Bench presses | 4 | 10, 10, 8, 8 |
| (5) Lateral raises | 3 | 10, 10, 8 |
| (6) Shoulder shrugs | 3 | 14, 12, 10 |
| (7) Upright rowing | 4 | 10, 10, 8, 8 |
| (8) Tricep curls | 4 | 10, 10, 8, 8 |
| (9) Bicep curls | 4 | 10, 10, 8, 8 |
| (10) Wrist curls | 3 | 12, 12, 10 |

# Pre-season training weekly planner

|  | January | February | March | April |
|---|---|---|---|---|
| *Monday* | Aerobic<br>Flexibility | Strength<br>Flexibility | Anaerobic<br>Flexibility | Flexibility<br>Nets<br>Fielding |
| *Tuesday* | Strength<br>Flexibility | Strength<br>Skills<br>Flexibility | Aerobic<br>Strength<br>Skills<br>Flexibility | Flexibility<br>Nets<br>Fielding<br>Circuit<br>maintenance |
| *Wednesday* | Aerobic | Anaerobic<br>Flexibility | Anaerobic<br>Flexibility | Flexibility<br>Match |
| *Thursday* | Strength<br>Flexibility | Strength<br>Skills<br>Flexibility | Strength<br>Skills<br>Flexibility | Flexibility<br>Nets<br>Fielding<br>Circuit<br>maintenance |
| *Friday* | Aerobic<br>Flexibility | Aerobic<br>Flexibility | Aerobic<br>Flexibility | Flexibility<br>Match |
| *Saturday* | Free (sport) | Free (sport) | Free (sport) | Match |
| *Sunday* | Rest | Rest | Rest | Rest |

# Fitness year planner (per week)

|  | January | February |
|---|---|---|
| *Aerobic* | – run 7 km (×3)<br>– cycle 1 hour (×3)<br>– swim 30 mins (×3) | – as January<br>– plus run 6×400 m (×2) |
| *Strength* | – weights: work on shoulders,<br>knees, back & ankles<br>– general programme | – as January |
| *Flexibility* | – yoga or stretching (×3) | – as January |
| *Skills* | – use video camera to analyse<br>techniques | – as January |

|  | **March** | **April** |
|---|---|---|
| *Aerobic* | – as February, but reduce all work to ×2<br>– plus run 6–10×50 m | – as March<br>– pre-season training ('cricket fitness') |
| *Strength* | – as February<br>– plus step or hill climbing (20 secs intervals) | – as March |
| *Flexibility* | – as February | – as March |
| *Skills* | – specific skills practice | – emphasis on fielding<br>– match build-up |

| **May** | **June–Sept.** | **October** | **November** | **December** |
|---|---|---|---|---|
| (1) Flexibility<br>(2) Match play<br>(3) Maintenance training<br>(4) Days off<br>(5) Fielding practice | SEASON IN PROGRESS | Rest period<br><br>Holiday with leisure activities | Light training<br><br>Running, cycling, swimming (×3) | Light training<br><br>Running, cycling, swimming (×3) |

(My thanks to Dr Ian Cockerill of Birmingham University for sharing with me his expertise in the field of cricket fitness. I am also grateful to Thierry Tison, Conrad Raine, Ken Davis, Darryl Foster and Mel Siff.)

# INDEX